STEPPING FORWARD

*Using Essential Oils to Support
a 12-Step Program*

Dr. Alia Kaneaiakala, Sheree Martin
& Benjamin Kaneaiakala III

STEPPING FORWARD
USING ESSENTIAL OILS TO SUPPORT A 12-STEP PROGRAM

iUniverse books may be ordered through booksellers or by contacting:

iUniverse
1663 Liberty Drive
Bloomington, IN 47403
www.iuniverse.com
1-800-Authors (1-800-288-4677)

ISBN: 978-1-5320-4566-0 (sc)
ISBN: 978-1-5320-4565-3 (e)

Print information available on the last page.

iUniverse rev. date: 07/06/2018

ESSENTIAL OILS AND THE 12 STEPS

Recovery from addiction may be achieved many different ways. However, it is important to use every potential tool of support because addiction is such a powerful force. It is highly encouraged that individuals embrace the 12 step program and find a sponsor, attend meetings regularly and work the steps. My experience in working in treatment and with individuals in recovery is that approaching the 12 steps is difficult for many and brings moments of hesitation or avoidance.

Working the 12 steps is difficult due to resistance both consciously and subconsciously. Individuals work through the experiences of both surrendering and acceptance. Taking inventory of past actions and harm upon others as well as addressing character defects are sometimes shameful or guilt ridden processes. Working the steps with a sponsor can make the difference in one's recovery and help clear out perspectives, memories or emotions that may lead an individual to relapse. Sometimes the addictive voice will encourage an individual to avoid the steps by creating different excuses or what the brain deceives one in believing to be rationalizations. Where the addictive voice is present or the subconscious links to the addiction, this becomes an important space for an individual to work the steps, not avoid them.

Using carefully chosen essential oils may be helpful for individuals to avoid the traps of the subconscious or addictive voice and aid in moving through the steps. Since oils are used both topically and via olfactory, they move into the limbic system within 20 seconds of use. The oils may support the resistance of sitting down to write or meditate on assignments linked to working a step as well as encourage staying engaged in the steps completely.

Having worked in the field of recovery for over a decade, I have learned it takes a village to battle addiction. I believe in utilizing anything potentially helpful to support the recovery process. I hope individuals will use the oils as they work through each step with their sponsor, in treatment and with a primary therapist. Oils may fill the gap between an individual being motivated to work the steps while simultaneously holding reservations regarding the program.

This manual will describe each essential oil and its correlation to each step. General information regarding essential oils is also provided for overall health and application.

Essential Oil Chemistry

Here is a brief introduction to the chemistry behind the powerful influence of aromas. The fragrance of an essential oil can directly affect everything from your emotional state to your lifespan.

The sense of smell is the ONLY sense that is directly linked to the Limbic System, which is the emotional center of your brain. Anxiety, fear, depression, anger and joy all emanate from this region. The Limbic System is also directly related to and can activate the Hypothalamus, which is one of the most important parts of the brain. It acts as our hormonal control center and releases hormones that affect many parts of the body.

Because of the unique molecular structure of essential oils, they can directly stimulate the Limbic System and the Hypothalamus. The inhalation of essential oils can be used to combat stress and emotional trauma and can also stimulate the production of hormones from the Hypothalamus.

So how does this work? Essential oils are the life blood of the plant. They deliver the nutrients to parts of the plant that it needs for survival, much like blood does in the human body. Essential oils have the ability to penetrate cell membranes and travel through the blood and the tissues. Essential Oils are made up of hundreds of constituents that are very similar to the make up of our cell membranes. When topically applied to the skin, they can work their way through the body within minutes. When inhaled, they can reach the limbic system in 20 seconds.

Emotional Patterns and Core Beliefs

Every individual has certain core beliefs that develop in childhood in relation to their environment and circumstances. Some core beliefs are positive such as "I am kind" or "I am smart" or "I am worthy". Some core beliefs are not as positive such as "I am invisible" or "I am unlovable" or "I am not important." These core beliefs develop in relation to important events and usually due to interpretations from primary people in our lives. These core beliefs are internalized due to the influence from important people and the timing. In essences, they develop with us as we grow.

Core beliefs are not in the forefront of our minds yet quietly exist with us and show up during pivotal moments. A person applying for a job or college may start to doubt their self and look for ways to avoid applying if their core belief has been "I am not smart" or "I am not good enough." In a way, we move through life with our core beliefs in tow. Some individuals work to prove that these core beliefs are not true. Someone who seeks success at a feverish pace may be trying to prove a core belief of "I am not important" is not true. Others may move through life finding evidence that the core belief is true as it may be too difficult to believe otherwise. With this idea, it stands to reason that individuals may get stuck in cycles of self-sabotage or perpetuating their worst fears coming true. When working the steps in recovery, individuals may get stuck on certain steps that challenge these core beliefs.

As core beliefs are deeply internalized, using essential oils may be a way to challenge core beliefs in a more experiential way. They may serve to help individuals challenge a core belief or emotional pattern through the senses and without old rationalizations or belief systems even knowing the oil is entering the limbic system. Essential oils may aid the process and release of old emotional patterns and allow a less defensive and more open space to receive positive belief patterns to replace old and unnecessary negative thoughts of self.

Clearing an Emotional Pattern

Dr. Carolyn L. Mein, a pioneer in health and nutrition, developed a process that uses essential oils to aid in clearing emotional patterns.

The struggles that many individuals encounter when working the steps is their conscious and subconscious resistance. Understanding how to clear an emotional pattern helps individuals to work through the emotions that accompany each step of recovery. Using essential oils supports minimizing the defenses and resistance that sometimes hides in the subconscious. To understand and meet the resistance of the subconscious, individuals need to find a different path, in which incorporating essential oils can be extremely helpful.

Accessing all areas of the body is necessary to clear an emotional pattern. Mental, emotional, spiritual and physical states all need to be addressed.

Mental: Acknowledgement of the pattern brings it to conscious awareness.

Emotional: Feeling both the positive and negative sides of the emotion will RELEASE the emotion.

Spiritual: Providing yourself with a "way out" by speaking a statement allows you to learn the lesson. This shifts the energy from the negative to the positive. Clearing a deep-seated emotional pattern requires replacing this pattern or feeling with a desired response. We learn to respond rather than react.

Physical: Applying the oil to the alarm and emotional points on the body accesses the physical, releasing the conditioned response that it held in our DNA and cellular memory. This is done by smelling the oil and applying it to the alarm points and the emotional points on the body.

Application frequency is determined by the depth of the emotional pattern. The length of time is up to the person. It may take 7 weeks or 7 months to clear a pattern. The more often you work on clearing the pattern, the quicker the results.

Along with applying the oils to points on the body, the oils can also be diffused in the bedroom at night. This allows the subconscious to continue working on the emotional clearing through the night.

If the emotional release becomes too intense, one can reduce the frequency and extend the time. Honor yourself and pay attention to what is best for you.

Clearing Procedure

1. Identify and feel the emotion
2. Smell the appropriate oil
3. Feel the other side of the emotion
4. Apply the oil to the alarm points
5. Apply the oil or touch the emotional points
6. Focus on or say the statement that provides a way out, moving you from a negative to a positive state
7. Repeat as needed.

STEP ONE

"We admitted we were powerless over alcohol – that our lives had become unmanageable."

Emotion: Powerless

Essential Oil – Highest Potential

Other Side: Powerful

Alarm Point - Kidney

Way out: I am empowered.

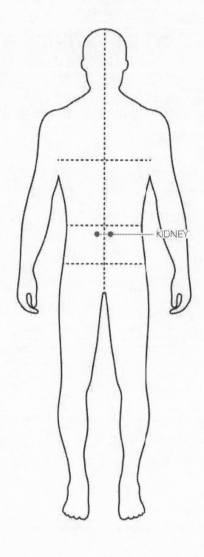

KIDNEY

Step One begins with admitting one is powerless and that life has become manageable. The complete admittance of such a vulnerable and humble state may be overwhelming for many. To add to the difficulty, if individuals have experienced trauma or unfortunately grew up with a need to be independent for the sake of survival, then step one pushes on what may have supported the individual's way of surviving. It may be difficult to work through step one in a deliberate and conscious way thus calling for the need of experiential help. Using the oil and by passing the conscious defenses, will ease the process of letting go of old beliefs and allow room for the individual to find an openness and support for new levels of vulnerability.

Supporting those who support recovery

The sensation of feeling powerless while watching a loved one struggle or suffer is unbearable. Applying the oil Highest Potential aids in maintaining a level of hope while simultaneously letting go of levels of control. Empowerment and taking agency is the ability to acknowledge how one may take steps forward effectively rather than fighting to control something like addiction that is bigger than any individual or family. The oils will serve to aid levels of anxiety with such a release and understanding that the individual in recovery is the only one who can do the work of sobriety. The use of the oil will offer a quieting of the anxiety and hopefully decrease the desire to step in and take over control.

STEP TWO

"Came to believe that a Power greater than ourselves could restore us to sanity."

Emotion: Resistance

Essential Oil – Surrender

Other Side: Openness

Alarm Point - Amygdala

Way out: I welcome change.

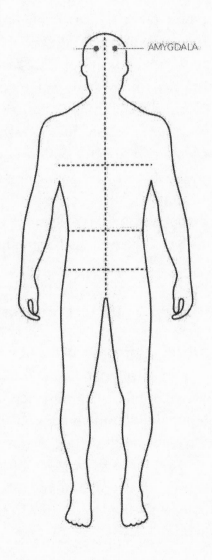

AMYGDALA

Step Two asks that individuals seek a higher power to help restore them to sanity. The connection to a higher power and believing in something bigger than ourselves is difficult for many individuals entering the recovery process. Many grew up without an attachment to religion or spirituality. Unfortunately, others saw many horrific scenes in their addiction that are difficult to understand within the concept of a higher power. During difficult moments, many individuals facing adversity may feel alone and disconnected making it a strain to understand the presence of a higher power. Many question where their higher power was in such moments or the existence of such an entity at all. The use of oils for step two will support the releasing of such ingrained beliefs and hopefully create space for the connection to a higher power if not at least the creation of room for the beginning of a relationship with something greater than ourselves.

Supporting those who support recovery

Step two requires that the loved one of the individual struggling with addiction is not responsible for their restoration and sobriety. Step two also nicely reminds the family member or loved one that they are also not alone in the process of recovery. The oil serves to keep individuals in the mode of surrender to sources greater than their own selves, to a higher power and to the community of recovery. Using the oil and acknowledging the welcoming of change will support the growth of all individuals impacted by addiction.

STEP THREE

"Made a decision to turn our will and our lives over to the care of God <u>as we understood Him.</u>"

Emotion: Oneness (Unconditional Love)

Essential Oil – Release

Other Side: Openness

Alarm Point - Amygdala

Way out: I welcome change.

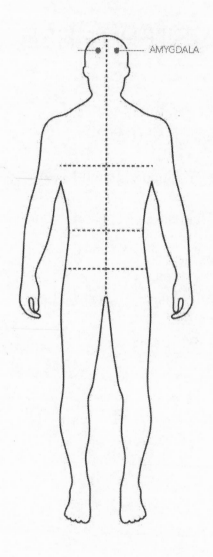

AMYGDALA

Step Three asks individuals to turn their will over to a God of their own understanding. Step two may challenge individuals to welcome a higher power while step three asks for a turning over of one's will. The oil chosen for this step encompasses unconditional love. Many individuals that find themselves in the throes of addiction have lost the sensation of unconditional love. Shame inhibits the ability to feel worthy of unconditional love due to the experiences of the addiction. Some may have not known an unconditional love in their childhood or lost those who best represented such a connection. Where it may feel impossible to step into unconditional love due to circumstances or irrational core beliefs, it becomes important to have the support of the oils to gently change the brain patterns. Through the limbic system, the oils create a new pathway allowing for a new understanding of being one with a higher power and positive components of self.

Supporting those who support recovery

The essential oil for this step is Release, continuing the process of surrender. For those individuals who lose many a night worrying about a loved one suffering with addiction, release is necessary for both emotional and physical health. Family members may have a habit of rescuing the individual in recovery and keep that pressure upon themselves. It will be helpful for family members to release this expectation and protect their own health and well-being. It may serve to be a powerful tool when trapped in worry and fear to use the oil to release such fears to a higher power and find a sense of peace.

STEP FOUR

"Made a searching and fearless moral inventory of ourselves."

Emotion: 1. Taking moral inventory.

2. Ability to cope and defensiveness

Essential Oil – 1. Sacred Mountain

2. Valor

Other Side: Openness

Alarm Point - Amygdala

Way out: I welcome change.

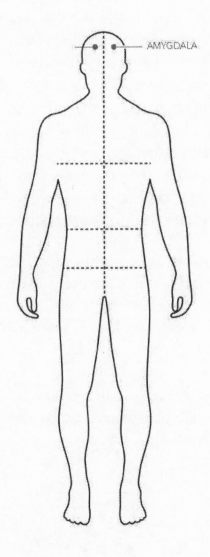

AMYGDALA

Step Four is where many individuals become stuck and stall while working the steps. I have witnessed many individuals that have completed steps one through three and then relapsed or stopped the process in potential avoidance of step four. Step four overwhelms many due to the extensiveness of creating an inventory of past hurts and the individuals involved. Many experience a fear of stepping into the past and looking at their part in hurtful experiences. As many individuals use substances to avoid difficult emotions and memories, step four is an overwhelming undertaking. Using oils while putting pen to paper and addressing step four will aid individuals being able to stay grounded to complete the work.

Supporting those who support recovery

Taking a fearless inventory, sometimes involves the loved ones of the individual to take on more than their share of the "blame" or reason for the addiction. Both of the oils assigned to this step are to offer a space to look at one's part in the journey openly and bravely and also offer a level of understanding while protecting against any shame that might arise. Acknowledgment and accountability are for growth and never for punishment and the essential oils will help maintain such a distinction.

STEP FIVE

"Admitted to God, to ourselves, and to another human being the exact nature of our wrongs."

Emotion: Repressed emotion, resistance to change, illusion

Essential Oil: Present Time (in the moment deal with the past)

Other Side: Speak out

Alarm Point: Sigmoid Colon

Way out: I am wanted and loveable.

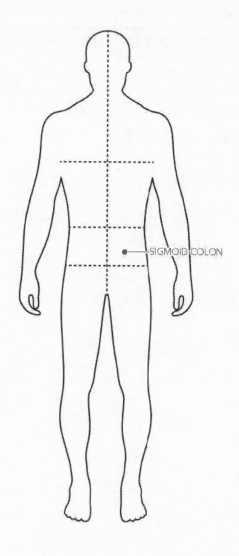

SIGMOID COLON

Step Five is an important part of the twelve step process. When Bill W. was writing the 12 steps, he consulted Carl Jung about the process. Jung suggested that individuals need to share their story with another human being, to be seen and understood for who they are in the present and for their past. It is important that this part of the process is without shame from the individual that receives the information to create safety. Using oils to increase safety during this vulnerable and anxiety- provoking process may be incredibly helpful.

Supporting those who support recovery

Step five is a powerful step and process to be seen and heard for our actions and past and still unconditionally accepted for that past. The essential oil, Present Time, supports individuals in finding a way to externalize their past from who they are currently known to be and focus on feeling unconditional love even in the midst of the battle against addiction.

STEP SIX

"Were entirely ready to have God remove all these defects of character."

Emotion: Feeling trapped

Essential oil: Transformation

Other side: Freedom

Alarm Point: Solar Plexus

Way Out: I am free.

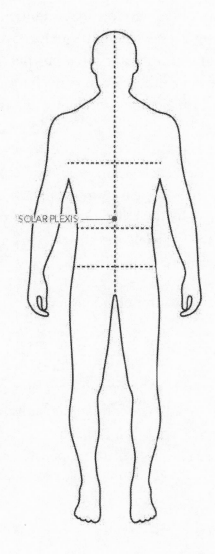

SOLAR PLEXIS

Step Six looks at defects of character. Oils may be helpful for individuals looking at defects of character with complete abandonment. It takes a level of bravery to see one's self with complete honesty and begin to work on character defects. Character defects often develop in childhood and serve as coping mechanisms. These defenses may serve to protect or help children deal with difficult situations but usually are not the most effective or healthiest coping mechanisms. Since such defenses develop during crucial developmental times, they tend to be internalized and difficult to abandon even when they no longer prove to be effective. Step Six allows individuals an opportunity to look at such defenses and determine how they are no longer effective and learn ways to release or replace such behaviors. Oils may be incredibly helpful in breaking past the internalized and life long defenses and offer an emotional space to release such defenses.

Supporting those who support recovery

Any character defects for those in recovery or individuals supporting recovery are difficult to address and release. Most character defects develop at young ages and are difficult to then remove without a better coping mechanism. The oils will help soften the process of looking at such character defects and encourage change. The oils will also support seeing others work to release character defects and not rescue them from the process.

STEP SEVEN

"Humbly asked Him to remove our shortcomings."

Emotion: Not good enough, less than

Essential Oil: Humility

Other Side: Acceptance

Alarm Point: Pericardium

Way Out: I express my best.

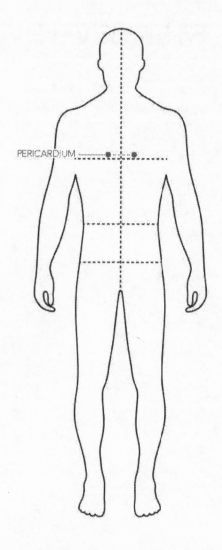

PERICARDIUM

Step Seven is a practice in humility. To ask one's Higher Power to remove shortcomings implies understanding from the previous step the depth of the shortcomings. Humility is found early on as individuals enter recovery and have recently escaped the "bottom" or close to "bottom" from their behaviors. As recovery continues, many individuals are eager to forget how bad their lives became while in the depths of addiction. The use of the oil with step seven supports remaining in humility and allowing the process of recovery, growth and connection to continue.

Supporting those who support recovery

The emotion of not good enough or feeling less than is nearly a constant for step seven for those working any type of recovery program, including Al-Anon. Many parents or spouses in particular may feel not good enough when their loved one struggles with addiction. Some may feel if they had been enough, the addiction would not have come to be and others may feel less than for not knowing how to respond. Still another option for loved ones, is feeling uncertain of their own self in their process of change. The oil, Humility supports acceptance of a process bigger than any one person. It encourages individuals to recognize all that can be expected of the self or another is authentic efforts to love and grow.

STEP EIGHT

"Made a list of all persons we have harmed and became willing to make amends to them all."

Emotion: Confined

Essential Oil: Envision

Other Side: Freedom

Alarm Point: Intuitive

Way Out: I allow myself to see.

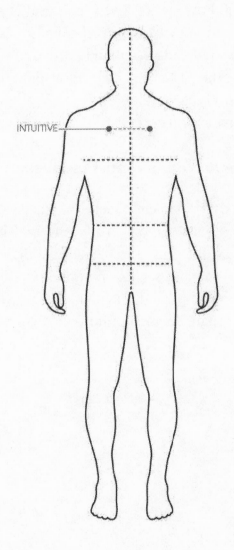

INTUITIVE

Step Eight is another stalling point for many while working the steps. To make a list of individuals harmed during their use or addiction is once again overwhelming and frightening. To think of each person that may have been impacted or harmed means simultaneously addressing negative events and choices. An oil will support the pen to the paper in creating the list and easing the anxiety, fear or dread of remembering and assessing the negative events of the past. The oil Envision allows a freedom to experience, feel and see without losing one's self in the process or the progress made in recovery.

Supporting those who support recovery

Using essential oils for step eight feels like a lucky coin in one's pocket or Dumbo with his feather for bravery. Envision is an incredible oil to be able to see a change not only in others but in one's self. Envision aids seeing and understanding a change to come in relationships and allowing the beginning of the imagination to prepare for such positive changes.

STEP NINE

"Make direct amends to such people wherever possible, except when to do so would injure them or others."

Emotion: Distrust, Past fear of repeating

Essential Oil: Forgiveness

Other Side: Trust

Alarm Point: Pancreas

Way Out: I have the courage to accept the truth.

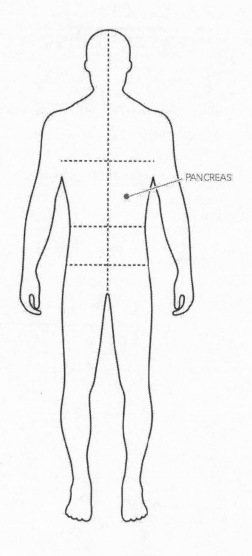

PANCREAS

Step Nine and the oil Forgiveness seem to naturally go hand in hand. Individuals may want to coat themselves in the oil of forgiveness when sitting down to make amends to others. Perhaps individuals may want to offer the oil to the person for whom the amends is owed to encourage a positive and peaceful environment. As one may hope for forgiveness from the person to who they owe an amends, the forgiveness is truly for the self. It is necessary to forgive the self, especially when an individual knows wholeheartedly that they would not repeat the behavior in sobriety or in the present.

Supporting those who support recovery

Step nine is the process of conversation about difficult topics in seeking understanding, clearance and forgiveness. Once again, using an essential oil, especially Forgiveness itself, serves to help the body and emotional self to feel supported in approaching conversations that may be nerve wracking and anxiety provoking otherwise. With the pancreas as the alarm point, a natural centering occurs due to the its location in the body. The oil and the location of the alarm point offers a grounding of sorts. This combination may offer support when having necessary conversations, removing concerns of the outcome of the exchange and focusing mainly on one's intentions of words.

STEP TEN

"Continued to take personal inventory and when we were wrong promptly admitted it."

Emotion: Insecurity to success

Essential Oil: Acceptance

Other Side: Success

Alarm Point: Ileum

Way out: I learn from all of life's experiences.

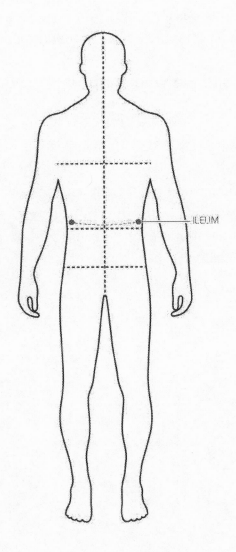

ILEUM

Step Ten aids the continuation of the process of taking an inventory. As individuals work the steps and continue in recovery, many learn that this is the foundation for their life and a beginning for change. Sobriety is the beginning and not the result. Using oils to support continue work on one's self and looking at behaviors in recovery for continued adaptation.

Supporting those who support recovery

Acceptance is key to growth. Rarely in life do we check off a box for our growth. Many individuals wish that self- growth and improvement could be simplified to a task and completion. True self-actualization is normally a process of continual growth which is maintained by staying attune to one's self and personal goals. Oils may support the ongoing process of meeting new challenges, changing behaviors and reinventing one's self in recovery.

STEP ELEVEN

"Sought through prayer and meditation to improve our conscious contact with God <u>as we understood Him</u>, praying only for knowledge of His will for us and the power to carry that out."

Emotion: Not safe to be me, in my body, in this world

Essential Oil: Gratitude

Other Side: Protected

Alarm Point: lower abdomen

Way Out: I am free to be me and to live in this world.

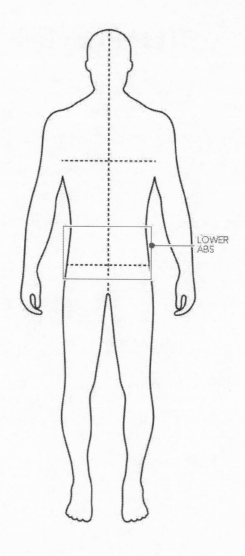

LOWER
ABS

Step Eleven focuses on continued contact with a higher power and employs the tools of meditation and prayer. This step supports recovery and continued growth in one's connection to their God and one's own higher self. Using oils will support the environment for the individual to continue in their spirituality and growth of understanding a bigger picture.

Supporting those who support recovery

The essential oil, Gratitude, supports creating a different sensation than the fear created by the impact of addiction. Gratitude allows for the acknowledgment of the positives that do exist, even when difficult to see or feel. Using the oil for meditation and prayer will aid the comfort of the space needed to be quiet within and hear one's connection to their higher power.

STEP TWELVE

"Having had a spiritual awakening as the result of these steps, we tried to carry this message to alcoholics, and to practice these principles in all our affairs."

Emotion: Connection Inter-dimensionally

Essential Oil: Awaken

Other Side: Wholeness

Alarm Point: Sacral Door

Way Out: I am complete.

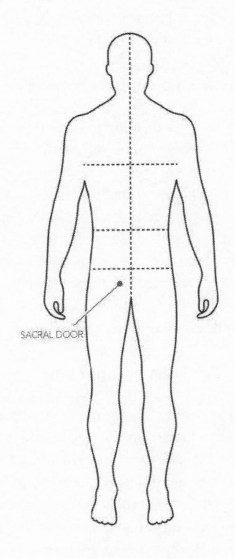

SACRAL DOOR

Step Twelve aims to continue the program and steps by having individuals carry the message and support others in the program. Such support aids connection on several levels and the use of oils for step twelve may keep individuals calm, connected and reminded of the work they have completed with their own 12 step process and share this process with others.

Supporting those who support recovery

The last oil for the twelve steps is Awaken. It seems fitting to encourage the internal changes from working a program of recovery and to acknowledge the sense of being complete. Addiction tends to rob those struggling as well as their families of any sense of feeling complete or whole. The voids created are locked in the past, present and try to penetrate the future. The oil of awaken aids seeing the addiction and its impact in more of its entirety to then see the process of recovery with more clarity. Awaken becomes an oil to continue to stay awake to any old feelings or reactions and stay present with each day.

Where many individuals may get stuck

With each of the twelve steps, individuals face different perspectives and components of the self. The process may be emotional, vulnerable and at times exhausting. Each person works through the steps at a different pace and may find different steps more challenging than others due to their own personal experiences. The use of the oils to help where one may become stagnant or have difficulty processing emotions that come up while working the step. Some might be downright avoidant of the step or process all together. The oils will support the purpose of each step as well as the overall process of working the steps.

This book and support of the oils has a universal applicability to anyone in a recovery process. The application of oils may support recovery in any category of addiction. The process of using oils may also be helpful to those healing from trauma, as grief support and for Post Traumatic Stress Disorder. The application and process with the oils may support individuals tackling anxiety and depression in the search of more peace and relief in their life. The path of the oils may offer support to a couple working to heal and support increased intimacy. Conversely, the layout of the oils may support someone healing over the loss of a relationship or another important relationship in their life. The purpose of this layout of oils is to support anyone on their own journey towards healing and growth.

The content in this protocol is very specific to Young Living Essential Oils and should not be used with oils from another source. Statements made in this protocol about Young Living Essential Oils have not been evaluated by the FDA. These products and information are not intended to diagnose, treat, cure or prevent any disease. Anyone suffering from disease or injury should consult with a physician.

Information found here is meant for educational and informational purposes only, and to motivate you to make your own health care and dietary decisions based upon your own research and in partnership with your health care provider. It should not be relied upon to determine dietary changes, a medical diagnosis or courses of treatment.

REFERENCE

Step One

Essential Oil – Highest Potential

Alarm Point - Kidney

Step Two

Essential Oil – Surrender

Alarm Point - Amygdala

Step Three

Essential Oil – Release

Alarm Point - Amygdala

Step Four

Essential Oil – 1. Sacred Mountain

2. Valor

Alarm Point - Amygdala

Step Five

Essential Oil: Present Time (in the moment deal with the past)

Alarm Point: Sigmoid Colon

Step Six

Essential oil: Transformation

Alarm Point: Solar Plexus

Step Seven

Essential Oil: Humility

Alarm Point: Pericardium

Step Eight

Essential Oil: Envision

Alarm Point: Intuitive

Step Nine

Essential Oil: Forgiveness

Alarm Point: Pancreas

Step Ten

Essential Oil: Acceptance

Alarm Point: Ileum

Step Eleven

Essential Oil: Gratitude

Alarm Point: Lower Abdomen

Step Twelve

Essential Oil: Awaken

Alarm Point: Sacral Door

REFERENCES

Young, N.D., Gary D. An Introduction to Young Living Essential Oils.

Essential Oils Desk Reference. Compiled by Essential Science Publishing, Sixth Edition, April 2014.

Releasing Emotional Patterns With Essential Oils by Carolyn L. Mein, D.C. Eleventh Edition, January 2014.